I0012103

Chapter 1: Introduction to Canva

- Understanding Canva's Mission and Purpose
- Exploring the Interface
- Setting Up Your Canva Account

Chapter 2: Getting Started with Canva Basics

- Creating Your First Design
- Choosing the Right Template
- Exploring the Design Tools
- Navigating Layers and Elements

Chapter 3: Design Principles for Beginners

- Introduction to Design Principles
- Understanding Color Theory
- Typography Essentials
- Utilizing Layouts and Composition

Chapter 4: Advanced Design Techniques

- Mastering Photo Editing
- Incorporating Illustrations and Icons
- Using Canva's Animation Features
- Creating Custom Graphics with Canva Pro

Chapter 5: Branding and Consistency

- Establishing Your Brand on Canva
- Creating Branded Templates
- Maintaining Consistency Across Designs

Chapter 6: Collaborating on Canva

- Team Collaboration Features
- Sharing and Presenting Designs
- Receiving and Providing Feedback

Chapter 7: Print and Digital Output

- Exporting Designs for Print
- Optimizing Designs for Social Media
- Creating Interactive PDFs

Chapter 8: Integrating Canva with Other Tools

- Importing and Exporting Files
- Using Canva with Design Software
- Integrating Canva with Marketing Platforms

Chapter 9: Tips and Tricks for Efficiency

- Keyboard Shortcuts
- Hidden Features
- Time-Saving Techniques

Chapter 10: Canva for Business and Marketing

- Leveraging Canva for Marketing Campaigns
- Designing Engaging Social Media Content
- Creating Eye-catching Presentations
- Designing Marketing Materials

Chapter 11: Troubleshooting and FAQs

- Common Issues and Solutions
- FAQs for Canva Users

Chapter 12: Staying Updated with Canva

- Exploring New Features
- Community and Support Resources
- Feedback and Suggestions

Conclusion:

- Recap of Key Takeaways
- Encouragement to Continue Exploring and Experimenting
- Inspiring Design Success Stories on Canva

Appendix:

- Glossary of Terms
- Additional Resources and References

This book aims to be a comprehensive guide for both beginners and experienced users, providing a thorough understanding of Canva's features and capabilities. Whether you're looking to enhance your personal projects or elevate your business's visual presence, "Mastering Canva" is designed to be a valuable resource for anyone wanting to unlock the full potential of this powerful design tool.

Chapter 1: Introduction to Canva

Welcome to the vibrant world of Canva, where creativity meets simplicity. In this chapter, we'll embark on a journey to understand the essence of Canva, its mission, and the incredible possibilities it offers for designing visually stunning graphics.

1.1 Unveiling Canva's Mission and Purpose

Discover the driving force behind Canva's inception and its commitment to empowering individuals, businesses, and organizations to express themselves visually. Explore the vision that fuels Canva's mission to democratize design, making it accessible to everyone, regardless of their design expertise.

1.2 Exploring the Interface

Dive into the user-friendly interface of Canva. Learn how to navigate effortlessly through the platform, from the creation of your account to the plethora of features available. Familiarize yourself with the intuitive layout, ensuring a seamless design experience right from the start.

1.3 Setting Up Your Canva Account

Unlock the full potential of Canva by setting up your personalized account. This section will guide you through the account creation process, helping you understand the advantages of having an account and the additional features it provides. Explore the various subscription options, including the free and premium plans, to tailor your Canva experience to your needs.

1.4 The Evolution of Canva

Take a brief journey through Canva's evolution, from its early days to the present. Explore key milestones, feature enhancements, and the company's commitment to continuous improvement. Gain insights into how user feedback has shaped the development of Canva into the versatile design platform it is today.

1.5 Canva's Impact on Design Culture

Delve into the impact Canva has had on the design landscape, influencing how individuals and businesses approach visual communication. Understand the role of Canva in fostering a culture of creativity, collaboration, and innovation, as well as its contribution to the rise of DIY design.

1.6 Embracing the Canva Community

Discover the vibrant Canva community, where creators, designers, and enthusiasts come together to share ideas, inspiration, and support. Learn about the various community forums, events, and resources that can enrich your Canva experience and connect you with like-minded individuals from around the world.

As we embark on this exploration of Canva, you'll gain a foundational understanding of the platform's roots, purpose, and the community that surrounds it. Whether you're a seasoned designer or a novice seeking to express your creativity, Canva is here to inspire and empower you on your design journey.

1.1 Understanding Canva's Mission and Purpose

Canva's mission goes beyond being just a design tool; it's a revolutionary force in making design accessible to all. The founders envisioned a world where creativity knows no boundaries, and everyone has the ability to express themselves visually. Canva's mission is grounded in the belief that design should not be exclusive to a select few with professional expertise; rather, it should be a skill accessible to individuals, businesses, educators, and non-profit organizations alike.

Explore the core values that drive Canva's mission, emphasizing inclusivity, empowerment, and innovation. Learn how Canva seeks to break down the barriers that traditionally hindered people from entering the world of design, fostering a global community of creators who can bring their ideas to life through visually compelling content.

1.2 Exploring the Interface

Canva's interface is a marvel of user-centric design, providing an intuitive and visually pleasing environment for users of all skill levels. Dive into the interface to discover its user-friendly layout, featuring drag-and-drop functionality, a vast library of design elements, and a seamless canvas for your creative projects.

Uncover the different sections of the interface, such as the sidebar with tools and elements, the workspace where your designs come to life, and the top menu that houses essential features. Understand how Canva's smart design grid and alignment tools assist in creating aesthetically pleasing compositions effortlessly. Whether you're a seasoned designer or a complete beginner, the interface is crafted to make your design journey enjoyable and efficient.

1.3 Setting Up Your Canva Account

To fully harness the power of Canva, setting up a personalized account is a pivotal step. Explore the step-by-step process of creating your account, including the option to sign up using your email, Google account, or Facebook profile. Delve into the benefits of having a Canva account, such as access to saved designs, collaboration features, and personalized recommendations.

Navigate through the different account plans, from the free tier that offers a wealth of design tools to the premium plans with additional features like unlimited storage, advanced collaboration options, and access to Canva Pro. Understand the flexibility and scalability of these plans, enabling you to tailor your Canva experience to match your specific needs, whether you're an individual creator or part of a larger team.

As you embark on your Canva journey, a solid understanding of its mission, interface, and the importance of setting up your account will pave the way for a fulfilling and creative experience on this dynamic design platform.

Chapter 2: Getting Started with Canva Basics

Welcome to the practical side of Canva! In this chapter, we'll roll up our sleeves and dive into the fundamental aspects of creating captivating designs.

2.1 Creating Your First Design

Let's embark on your creative journey by learning the ropes of crafting your very first design on Canva. From selecting the canvas size to adding elements and customizing text, we'll explore the step-by-step process of bringing your ideas to life. Understand the importance of the blank canvas as your playground and discover how easy it is to translate your vision into a visually appealing design.

2.2 Choosing the Right Template

Templates are the unsung heroes of design efficiency. Explore the vast library of Canva templates tailored for various purposes, from social media posts to business presentations. Learn how to sift through the multitude of options, selecting the template that aligns with your project goals. Uncover the versatility of these pre-designed layouts, providing a solid foundation for your creativity while saving you valuable time.

2.3 Exploring the Design Tools

Canva's toolbox is a treasure trove of design features that cater to both beginners and seasoned designers. Delve into the diverse array of design tools, including text manipulation, image cropping, and color adjustment. Gain insights into the power of the Canva Pro tools, offering advanced functionalities like background remover, animation, and custom font uploads. By the end of this section, you'll be equipped with the knowledge to navigate the tools confidently, turning your ideas into polished designs.

2.4 Navigating Layers and Elements

Understanding the concept of layers is fundamental to mastering Canva's design environment. Unpack the intricacies of layer management, exploring how to arrange, group, and lock elements on your canvas. Learn the importance of organizing your design elements effectively, ensuring a smooth workflow and easy editing. Whether you're working on a simple social media post or a complex presentation, mastering layers and elements is the key to creating professional-looking designs with precision.This chapter is your gateway to the practical side of Canva. By grasping the essentials of creating designs, selecting templates, exploring design tools, and navigating layers, you'll be well-prepared to unleash your creativity and make the most out of this dynamic design platform. Let's turn those ideas into visually stunning realities!

Chapter 3: Design Principles for Beginners

Design is not just about aesthetics; it's about conveying a message effectively and creating a visual language that resonates with your audience. In this chapter, we'll explore the foundational principles that underpin successful design.

3.1 Introduction to Design Principles

Embark on your design journey by understanding the core principles that govern the world of design. Explore concepts such as balance, contrast, unity, and hierarchy, and learn how these principles form the backbone of visually appealing compositions. Whether you're a novice or an experienced designer, grasping these fundamentals will elevate your designs to new heights.

3.2 Understanding Color Theory

Color is a powerful tool in the designer's arsenal. Dive into the realm of color theory, where you'll discover the emotional impact of different hues and how to create harmonious color palettes. Explore the psychological aspects of color, its cultural significance, and the practical application of color theory to evoke specific moods and convey your message effectively.

3.3 Typography Essentials

Typography is more than just choosing a font; it's about making your text visually engaging and easy to read. Uncover the essentials of typography, from font selection and spacing to hierarchy and alignment. Learn how to pair fonts effectively and use text as a design element to enhance the overall aesthetic of your creations. By mastering typography, you'll be able to communicate your message with clarity and style.

3.4 Utilizing Layouts and Composition

The way elements are arranged on a canvas significantly impacts the overall design. Delve into the art of layouts and composition, exploring grid systems, alignment, and the rule of thirds. Understand how to create focal points, guide the viewer's eye, and establish a sense of visual hierarchy. Whether you're designing a poster, social media graphic, or presentation slide, mastering layout and composition will bring cohesiveness to your designs.

By the end of this chapter, you'll have a solid understanding of design principles, color theory, typography essentials, and the nuances of layouts and composition. Armed with this knowledge, you'll be well-equipped to infuse your designs with creativity, purpose, and a professional touch. Design is not just about making things look good; it's about making them work effectively, and these principles will be your guide.

Chapter 4: Advanced Design Techniques

Now that you've laid the foundation with design principles, let's delve into the realm of advanced techniques that will take your Canva designs to the next level.

4.1 Mastering Photo Editing

Unleash the full potential of your images with advanced photo editing techniques in Canva. Explore features like filters, adjustments, and effects to enhance the visual appeal of your photos. Learn to retouch and manipulate images seamlessly, transforming ordinary pictures into captivating works of art. This section will guide you through the intricacies of Canva's photo editing tools, providing you with the skills to create professional-looking visuals.

4.2 Incorporating Illustrations and Icons

Elevate your designs by incorporating custom illustrations and icons. Explore Canva's extensive library of graphics or learn to upload and integrate your own. Understand the principles of iconography and illustration, and discover how these elements can enhance the storytelling aspect of your designs. Whether you're creating a logo, infographic, or social media post, mastering the art of incorporating illustrations and icons will add a unique and personalized touch to your creations.

4.3 Using Canva's Animation Features

Bring your designs to life with animation. Explore Canva's animation features and learn to add movement to elements, creating engaging and dynamic visuals. Understand the principles of timing, transitions, and effects to craft animations that captivate your audience. Whether you're designing presentations, social media content, or interactive graphics, this section will guide you through the process of adding that extra spark to your designs.

4.4 Creating Custom Graphics with Canva Pro

Unlock the advanced features of Canva Pro to create custom graphics tailored to your unique needs. Dive into the world of resizable designs, transparent backgrounds, and advanced export options. Explore the magic of the background remover tool, enabling you to seamlessly integrate your designs into various contexts. This section will empower you to push the boundaries of creativity, providing you with the tools to craft sophisticated and professional graphics with Canva Pro.

By exploring these advanced design techniques, you'll gain the skills and knowledge needed to create visually stunning and dynamic content in Canva. Whether you're a business professional, content creator, or aspiring designer, these techniques will open up a world of creative possibilities, allowing you to express your ideas with precision and flair.

Chapter 5: Branding and Consistency

In the world of design, establishing a strong brand presence and maintaining consistency are crucial elements that contribute to the success and recognition of your content. This chapter focuses on the strategic aspects of branding and how Canva can be utilized to build and sustain a cohesive visual identity.

5.1 Establishing Your Brand on Canva

Dive into the process of bringing your brand identity to life within Canva. Learn to incorporate your brand colors, fonts, and logo seamlessly into your designs. Explore Canva's Brand Kit feature, allowing you to centralize and manage all your brand assets in one place. Understand the importance of aligning your designs with your brand personality, ensuring that every piece of content represents your brand accurately.

5.2 Creating Branded Templates

Efficiency meets consistency with the creation of branded templates. Uncover the power of designing templates that reflect your brand aesthetics, enabling you and your team to produce on-brand content effortlessly. Learn how to customize and save templates for various purposes, from social media posts to presentations. Dive into the world of Canva Pro's template locking feature, ensuring that brand guidelines are adhered to consistently across all your designs.

5.3 Maintaining Consistency Across Designs

Consistency is key to building brand recognition. Explore strategies for maintaining a cohesive look and feel throughout your designs, whether they are created by you, your team, or collaborators. Understand the importance of consistent use of brand elements, layout choices, and messaging. Dive into Canva's collaboration features, discovering how to ensure that every design produced aligns with the established brand guidelines. This section will empower you to uphold a professional and recognizable brand image across all your visual content.

By mastering the art of branding and consistency within Canva, you'll not only streamline your design process but also strengthen your brand identity. Whether you're a solo entrepreneur, part of a small business, or a member of a larger organization, these principles will guide you in creating designs that resonate with your audience and contribute to the overall success of your brand.

Chapter 6: Collaborating on Canva

Design is often a collaborative process, and Canva recognizes the importance of fostering teamwork and facilitating seamless collaboration. In this chapter, we'll explore the collaborative features of Canva that empower individuals and teams to work together efficiently.

6.1 Team Collaboration Features

Unlock the potential of collaborative design by delving into Canva's team collaboration features. Explore the creation and management of teams within Canva, allowing multiple users to collaborate on projects seamlessly. Understand the role of shared folders, enabling teams to organize and access designs collectively. Learn about real-time collaboration, where team members can simultaneously work on a design, making the creative process dynamic and interactive.

6.2 Sharing and Presenting Designs

Discover the various ways you can share and present your designs within Canva. Explore the option to share designs directly with team members, clients, or stakeholders. Learn about the versatility of sharing links, enabling recipients to view or edit designs based on your preferences. Dive into the presentation mode, allowing you to showcase your designs in a professional and engaging manner. Whether you're collaborating internally or presenting your work externally, Canva provides a range of tools to make sharing and presenting designs a seamless experience.

6.3 Receiving and Providing Feedback

Effective collaboration involves clear communication and feedback. Learn how to leverage Canva's commenting and annotation features to receive and provide feedback on designs. Explore the ability to leave comments directly on specific elements, making collaboration more precise and efficient. Understand how version history can be used to track changes and revert to previous iterations if needed. This section will guide you in creating a collaborative design environment where feedback flows seamlessly, fostering a culture of continuous improvement.

By mastering the collaborative features of Canva, you'll be able to work seamlessly with your team, clients, or collaborators, whether you're in the same office or continents apart. These collaborative tools not only enhance communication but also streamline the design workflow, ensuring that everyone involved can contribute their expertise to create visually compelling and impactful designs.

Chapter 7: Print and Digital Output

As a designer, your creations may find their way to various platforms, both in print and across digital landscapes. In this chapter, we'll explore how Canva can be leveraged to optimize and export designs for diverse outputs.

7.1 Exporting Designs for Print

Dive into the intricacies of preparing your designs for print. Explore the export options within Canva, ensuring that your designs meet the specifications required for professional printing. Learn about resolution, color modes, and bleed settings to guarantee high-quality print results. Understand how to export designs in popular print-ready file formats, ensuring that your creations look just as stunning on paper as they do on your screen.

7.2 Optimizing Designs for Social Media

In the age of social media, optimizing your designs for online platforms is essential. Explore the specific considerations for social media graphics, including image dimensions, aspect ratios, and file sizes. Learn how to leverage Canva's social media templates and resizing tools to adapt your designs for various platforms such as Instagram, Facebook, Twitter, and more. This section will empower you to create visually appealing and shareable content that stands out in the digital landscape.

7.3 Creating Interactive PDFs

Unlock the potential of interactive PDFs to elevate your digital documents. Explore Canva's features for creating interactive elements within PDFs, such as hyperlinks, buttons, and multimedia. Learn how to design engaging presentations, portfolios, or digital brochures that captivate your audience with interactive elements. Whether you're creating content for business, education, or personal projects, this section will guide you in leveraging the dynamic capabilities of interactive PDFs within Canva.

By understanding how to export designs for both print and digital outputs, you'll ensure that your creations shine across various mediums. Whether you're producing materials for physical distribution or sharing content online, Canva provides the tools and flexibility to adapt your designs for diverse platforms, allowing you to reach your audience effectively in both the tangible and virtual realms.

Chapter 8: Integrating Canva with Other Tools

Efficiency in design often involves seamless integration with other tools and platforms. In this chapter, we'll explore how Canva can be integrated into your broader workflow, connecting with various tools and software to enhance your design capabilities.

8.1 Importing and Exporting Files

Learn the art of importing and exporting files to and from Canva. Understand how to bring external elements into your designs by importing images, illustrations, and data. Explore the export options to ensure compatibility with other software or to create backups of your work. Whether you're collaborating with other designers, working on multiple platforms, or incorporating external resources, mastering file import and export functionalities in Canva is crucial for a seamless design workflow.

8.2 Using Canva with Design Software

Discover the synergy between Canva and other design software. Learn how to integrate Canva seamlessly into your existing design toolkit, whether you're using Adobe Creative Cloud, Sketch, or other popular design software. Understand the benefits of cross-platform compatibility and how to enhance your workflow by incorporating Canva's user-friendly interface and collaborative features alongside your preferred design tools.

8.3 Integrating Canva with Marketing Platforms

Explore the strategic integration of Canva with marketing platforms to streamline your promotional efforts. Learn how to design content directly within Canva and seamlessly integrate it with marketing tools such as Mailchimp, HubSpot, or social media scheduling platforms. Understand the benefits of maintaining a cohesive design and marketing workflow, ensuring that your visual content aligns seamlessly with your broader marketing strategy.

By mastering the integration of Canva with other tools, you'll enhance your efficiency and expand your design capabilities. Whether you're working with external files, incorporating Canva into your existing design software ecosystem, or integrating it with marketing platforms, this chapter will guide you in creating a holistic and streamlined design process that aligns with your broader creative and strategic goals.

Chapter 9: Tips and Tricks for Efficiency

In the fast-paced world of design, efficiency is key. This chapter is dedicated to unveiling a collection of tips and tricks that will turbocharge your Canva workflow, saving you time and enhancing your overall efficiency.

9.1 Keyboard Shortcuts

Navigate Canva like a pro by mastering keyboard shortcuts. Explore a comprehensive list of shortcuts that cover everything from basic navigation to advanced design functions. Learn how to speed up your workflow, switch between tools, and execute commands with the tap of a key. By incorporating keyboard shortcuts into your design routine, you'll find yourself working faster and more intuitively within Canva.

9.2 Hidden Features

Unlock the full potential of Canva by uncovering its hidden gems. Explore features that may be tucked away in menus or less apparent on the surface. From advanced editing options to unique design elements, this section will guide you through lesser-known features that can add flair and functionality to your designs. Discover the power of these hidden tools and how they can elevate your creative process.

9.3 Time-Saving Techniques

Efficiency is not just about speed but also about smart workflows. Dive into time-saving techniques that can streamline your design process. Learn how to leverage templates effectively, organize your workspace for optimal productivity, and use Canva's features to automate repetitive tasks. This section is filled with strategies to help you work smarter, allowing you to focus more on the creative aspects of your designs.

By incorporating these tips and tricks into your Canva toolkit, you'll become a more efficient and confident designer. Whether you're a beginner looking to enhance your skills or an experienced designer aiming to optimize your workflow, this chapter is designed to empower you with the knowledge to navigate Canva with ease and efficiency.

Chapter 10: Canva for Business and Marketing

In this chapter, we'll explore how Canva can be a powerhouse for business and marketing endeavors. Discover how to leverage its features to create compelling marketing campaigns, engaging social media content, impactful presentations, and eye-catching marketing materials.

10.1 Leveraging Canva for Marketing Campaigns

Uncover the strategies for utilizing Canva in your marketing campaigns. Learn how to create visually appealing and effective marketing materials such as posters, flyers, and banners. Explore Canva's tools for A/B testing, enabling you to refine your designs based on audience response. Whether you're promoting a product, event, or brand, this section will guide you in leveraging Canva to create marketing collateral that captures attention and drives engagement.

10.2 Designing Engaging Social Media Content

Social media is a visual playground, and Canva is your toolkit for creating content that stands out. Explore the intricacies of designing engaging and shareable social media graphics. Learn how to optimize your designs for different platforms, use eye-catching visuals, and incorporate branding consistently. Whether you're running a social media campaign or simply enhancing your online presence, Canva is your go-to platform for crafting content that resonates with your audience.

10.3 Creating Eye-catching Presentations

In the world of business, presentations are a powerful tool for communication. Discover how Canva can elevate your presentation game. Learn the art of designing slides that are not only informative but also visually captivating. Explore templates, layout options, and interactive elements that make your presentations memorable. Whether you're pitching a project, delivering a keynote, or conducting a training session, Canva can transform your slides into a compelling visual narrative.

10.4 Designing Marketing Materials

From business cards to brochures, Canva is equipped to assist you in crafting diverse marketing materials. Explore the versatility of the platform for designing materials that leave a lasting impression. Learn how to customize templates for print and digital distribution, ensuring consistency across various mediums. This section will guide you in creating marketing materials that align with your brand and effectively communicate your message to your target audience.

By harnessing the power of Canva for business and marketing purposes, you'll be equipped to create impactful campaigns, enhance your online presence, deliver compelling presentations, and produce marketing materials that leave a lasting impression. This chapter serves as a guide to unlocking the full potential of Canva in the dynamic and competitive landscape of business and marketing.

Chapter 11: Troubleshooting and FAQs

Even the smoothest design process may encounter bumps along the way. In this chapter, we'll address common issues users may face while using Canva and provide answers to frequently asked questions to ensure a seamless design experience.

11.1 Common Issues and Solutions

Explore a troubleshooting guide that addresses common challenges. users may encounter on Canva. From technical glitches to design-related obstacles, this section will provide solutions and workarounds to keep your creative process flowing smoothly. Whether you're facing issues with file exports, collaborative features, or tool functionalities, this troubleshooting guide will empower you to overcome obstacles and continue creating with confidence.

11.2 FAQs for Canva Users

Delve into a curated list of frequently asked questions that encompass various aspects of Canva usage. From account management to design tips, these FAQs provide quick and insightful answers to common queries. Whether you're a beginner seeking clarity on basic functionalities or an experienced user looking for advanced tips, this section serves as a comprehensive resource to address the most common inquiries posed by Canva users.

By understanding the solutions to common issues and having quick access to answers for frequently asked questions, you'll be better equipped to navigate potential challenges and optimize your Canva experience. This chapter aims to serve as a handy reference, ensuring that users of all levels can troubleshoot effectively and find solutions to any hurdles encountered while utilizing the versatile features of Canva.

Chapter 12: Staying Updated with Canva

In the ever-evolving landscape of design tools, staying updated with the latest features, resources, and community engagement is crucial. This chapter is dedicated to guiding users on how to remain informed and involved with the continuous enhancements offered by Canva.

12.1 Exploring New Features

Discover how to keep abreast of the latest features and updates rolled out by Canva. Learn where to find release notes, update logs, and announcements from the Canva team. Explore the process of exploring and incorporating new tools and functionalities into your design workflow. Staying updated on the latest features ensures that you can leverage the full potential of Canva and take advantage of new tools that enhance your creative process.

12.2 Community and Support Resources

Uncover the wealth of support and community resources available within the Canva ecosystem. Learn how to engage with the Canva community, from forums and discussion groups to social media channels. Explore support resources, including FAQs, help articles, and customer support options. By tapping into the Canva community and support infrastructure, you can enhance your learning experience, troubleshoot effectively, and connect with fellow designers.

12.3 Feedback and Suggestions

Understand how to provide feedback and suggestions to Canva, contributing to the ongoing improvement of the platform. Explore the various channels through which users can share their thoughts, report issues, and suggest enhancements. Learn about the importance of user feedback in shaping the future of Canva and how your input can directly influence the evolution of the platform.

By staying updated with Canva, you not only ensure that you are working with the latest and greatest tools but also actively contribute to the improvement of the platform. Whether you're exploring new features, engaging with the community, or providing feedback, this chapter is your guide to staying connected with Canva's vibrant ecosystem and remaining at the forefront of design innovation.

Conclusion: Mastering Canva - Unleashing Your Creative Potential

Congratulations on completing this comprehensive journey through the diverse world of Canva! As you reflect on the insights gained from each chapter, let's recap some key takeaways and encourage you to continue your exploration and experimentation.

Recap of Key Takeaways

Design Principles: Understand the fundamentals of design principles, color theory, typography, and layout to create visually compelling and effective designs.

Advanced Techniques: Dive into advanced design techniques, from photo editing to animation, and explore the creative possibilities with Canva Pro.

Branding and Consistency: Establish a strong brand presence by incorporating your brand elements and maintaining consistency across all designs.

Collaboration: Leverage Canva's collaborative features to work seamlessly with teams, share designs, and provide and receive feedback efficiently.

Print and Digital Output: Optimize your designs for print and digital platforms, ensuring they look stunning whether in physical or virtual spaces.

Integration with Other Tools: Integrate Canva into your workflow by importing and exporting files, using it alongside other design software, and connecting it with marketing platforms.

Efficiency Tips: Boost your efficiency with keyboard shortcuts, hidden features, and time-saving techniques, allowing you to work smarter, not harder.

Canva for Business and Marketing: Harness Canva's power for marketing campaigns, social media content, presentations, and various marketing materials to elevate your business strategies.

Troubleshooting and FAQs: Equip yourself with solutions to common issues and answers to frequently asked questions for a smooth design experience.

Staying Updated with Canva: Stay informed about new features, engage with the community for support, and contribute your feedback to shape the future of Canva.

Encouragement to Continue Exploring and Experimenting

The world of design is dynamic and ever-changing. As you conclude this guide, we encourage you to embrace a mindset of continuous exploration and experimentation. Canva evolves, and so should your creative approach. Dive into new features, try out different design styles, and push your creative boundaries. The more you experiment, the more you'll discover about your own design preferences and capabilities.

Inspiring Design Success Stories on Canva

To inspire you further, take a moment to explore success stories of individuals and businesses that have achieved remarkable results using Canva. From startups creating impactful branding to social media influencers connecting with their audience through visually stunning content, these stories highlight the transformative potential of Canva across various industries.

Remember, your design journey is unique, and Canva is here to empower your creativity. Whether you're a seasoned designer or just starting, the possibilities are endless. Embrace the creative freedom Canva offers, and let your imagination soar.

Happy designing!

www.ingramcontent.com/pod-product-compliance
Lightning Source LLC
La Vergne TN
LVHW051634050326
832903LV00033B/4758